Colombian Killers

The True Stories of the Three Most Prolific Serial Killers on Earth

Ryan Green

Luis Alfredo Garavito
Pedro Alonzo Lopez
Daniel Camargo Barbosa

ISBN-13: 978-1523938612
ISBN-10: 1523938617

CONTENTS

Introduction 7

The Making of Murderers 9

Luis Alfredo Garavito: 'La Bestia' 11

Early Life and Motivational Evolution 12

The Hunt: Discovery and Chase...17

The Arrest: Unmasking the Man.. 22

Due Process: The Road to Conviction..................................... 28

True Crime: Victimology and Methodology 33

Pedro Alonzo Lopez: 'The Monster of the Andes' 35

The Making of a Monster...36

The State vs Lopez: The Discovery and Chase 40

The Unveiling of a Madman 44

The Law of the Land: Conviction and Beyond 47

The Psychology of a Psychopath 52

Daniel Camargo Barbosa: 'The Sadist of El Charquito'.....56

The Creation of Camargo..57

Inside the Mind of a Murderer... 63

The Evolution of a Murderer..67

The Pursuit of a Psychopath: Chase and Capture 71

Imprisonment and Death 76

Conclusion...**78**

About the Author 79

Another Title by Ryan Green 80

Introduction

Even in today's jaded society, the taking of a human life strikes us as an utterly chilling act. It is the permanence of death, the finality of it that terrifies us. Horrifying as it may seem, the blood-curdling truth is that for some men, one murder is not the end. Instead, it is almost as if that first murder opens of the flood gates through which pours the torrent of carnage wrought by men such as Ted Bundy, Ed Gein, and Jack the Ripper.

There is however, a side of Hell so dark even monsters such as Bundy would shrink from it.

Colombian Killers is a look into the minds that lie beneath the madness. The stories of three men who have forever tainted the lush fields of Latin America with a horror that spans three decades of civil war are here brought to light. This book narrates the sadistic acts of Luis Alfredo Garavito, Pedro Alonzo Lopez, and Daniel Camargo Barbosa.

For these men, rape, and murder were but the beginning of the horrors they inflicted upon the world. The fear their crimes inspire is not about their nature, the methodology, or even the victims. It is about who the killers themselves are.

This book begins with three parts, each dedicated to one of these three monsters of modern-day Colombia. Once you've been edified with the general knowledge of the atrocities, we will delve further into the tiny details, the forgotten horrors, the thousands of ways that we as a society failed these men and, in so doing, shaped them into be the monsters they are known as today.

Luis Garavito, Pedro Lopez, and Daniel Barbosa are among the most prolific serial killers in the world. Between them, they were convicted of 329 murders, but it's believed that the number they committed is over 750. This book is not for the faint of heart, nor for the feeble of spirit. Be very sure you want to know what you are about to read, because if you can be sure of nothing else, be sure of this: You will never forget what you are about to read.

The Making of Murderers

To begin with, let's talk about the term 'serial killer.' The very notion of a 'serial killer' has alternately appalled and captivated the human race for generations. For as morbidly fascinating as we may find Hannibal Lecter, the thought of such a character prowling the streets is enough to make us walk just a little faster as we head home.

So why do the most evil, sub-human villains of human society become such natural celebrities? Why are *we*, the supposedly normal members of the human race, so in thrall to the horrors that such people threaten to visit upon the careful constructs of our normal, unaffected lives?

The way one NYPD Homicide Detective puts it, '*The why is the wow.*' To elaborate, our macabre fascination comes in part the shock of such acts--the sheer insanity of them, the horror of the possibility of such a thought crossing our own minds, is what truly enthrals us. In our 'normal' world, the 'why' behind all of these murders demonstrates to us how different, how singular, these distant monsters are, while simultaneously forcing us to admit, in the deepest corners of our minds, by way of something as mundane as a bowl of cereal or a favourite movie, just how much they are *not*.

It is this vacuum between conventional and inexplicable that we seek to fill. And so, it is that desire that brings us to where we are now, attempting to decipher the minds of monsters depraved enough to have earned a title more sinister than mere 'murderer.' We speak, of course, of 'serial killers.' A serial killer is a soul who has been driven to the most unspeakable of crimes, not just once, and not just in a fit of rage–but gradually, over a period of time, at least two to three times, driven by a need, be it sexual, rage-fuelled, power-based, or constructed around the thrill of some perverse psychological gratification.

The men we will be discussing are motivated by perhaps the most chilling trifecta--sex, power and revenge.

Luis Alfredo Garavito: 'La Bestia'

Early Life and Motivational Evolution

'What do you want to be when you grow up?'

A clichéd question, asked of nearly every child. An easy question with anything but an easy answer. For all the million answers children have given to this question over time, the answer is never 'remorseless paedophilic mass murderer.' It's unlikely that these individuals were born with this intention. To commit such atrocities, an individual must have encountered numerous or significant damaging events in his or her life.

Luis Alfredo Garavito Cubilos, known as 'La Bestia' (The Beast), Tribilín (Disney's Goofy), 'El Cura' (The Priest), or 'Bonifacio Morera Lizcano,' was born in the small village of Génovo in Quindio of Colombia on the 25th of January, 1957, a few months before the deposition of President Gustavo Rojas and at the threshold of a decade-long civil war that would ravage the country. He was the son of Rosa Delia and Manuel Antoni, the first of seven children, to be followed by three brothers and three sisters. He lived a relatively impoverished childhood and was subjected to frequent abuse. Psychologists have been quick to attribute to Luis the three characteristics that define most sexually driven serial killers: acceptance seeking, repressed hostility, and incompatibility amongst peers--or narcissism, sadism, and loneliness.

While this trifecta is what many claim drive the average 'lust killer'--each of these traits also stands individually as a marker of the desperation that can fuel serial murderers, especially when they are imbedded in one at such a young age.

Defining these traits allows us not only to identify individual aspects of personality development, but to do so while directly tying them in with the hedonistic urges (or in this specific case, isolative rejection) as well as physical, emotional and sexual abuse that drove Luis Garavito to become what he became.

Narcissism

It has been widely theorized that, of the factors that affect most organized serial killers such as Luis Garavito, the one that acts as the catalyst for all other factors is malignant narcissism. Garavito was born a healthy first-born son in an impoverished Colombian family in the middle of a civil war that was decades long. He was, as such, the perfect child. His own sense of self would have thus been built up considerably into an almost overwhelming sense of self-worth.

Unfortunately for Garavito, such a sense of self-worth is as fragile as it is formidable, making it easily disturbed. For Garavito, the affronts to his fragile self-worth would come in the form of his six younger siblings, making it seem almost as if he was usurped six times over and replaced at least three times.

Coupled with this struggle was the physical abuse Garavito suffered at the hands of his father and the sexual abuse he suffered at the hands of his two neighbours--actions that caused him to develop within himself a frustrated neurosis in terms of parental ideals. He was betrayed in the worst possible ways by those who were meant to protect him. It was from this moment that his fixation with his own age at the time (seen later in terms of victimology) and the fiduciary relationships he had formed during that time period began to solidify as a perverted power struggle.

The abuse occurred when Garavito was about 12 0r 13 years old, an age when he was still naïve enough to think he was invincible, as most children that age do.

The primary projection of his narcissism, first damaged with the shifting of family dynamics as the other siblings were born and then shattered conclusively with the abuse he was subjected to, likely acted as a key motivator not just of his murders but, more specifically, his replication of the sexual abuse he suffered at the hands of 'trusted' parent figures.

Sadism

Unlike Pedro Lopez, Luis Garavito's methodology speaks of a vastly different kind of sadism. Garavito's style was simple: he would rape first and then disembowel or slit the throats of his victims. Death came after the act of rape, not as a part of it. This indicates that Garavito had a Sadistic Personality Disorder rather than a proclivity for Sexual Sadism. His murders were not sexually motivated, but rather undertaken because he enjoyed the sense of God-like power the psychological and physical suffering of other's brought him.

For Garavito, the act of sex was tainted with the abuse he suffered at the hands of his neighbours--parental figures whom he trusted-- leading to his repetition of the act with his victims. Garavito did not leave his victims alive to suffer through what he had suffered through. In his mind, to do so would have been an act of mercy or, as is more likely, a relinquishing of power.

One of the key motivators of sadistic murders is the basic need for control. For Garavito, who as a child continuously felt wrongly usurped, the cruelty of sadism was likely manifested in the way he tortured most victims after the rape, as an ultimate show of dominance before the final act of murder.

Loneliness

As simplistic as it may sound, loneliness is the thing that link sadism and narcissism--these two things representing the two more volatile sides of the deranged mind of Luis Garavito. Garavito's childhood was, in its own way, solitary to the extreme.

He was born a firstborn son, only to be continuously challenged for his position in the household, circumstances which made him go from the centre of attention to the least significant, in terms of need. When this loneliness was further triggered triggered by at first neglect, and then abuse, Garavito's fundamental existence became a matter of question-- who was he outside of his identity as the oldest son? What would he amount to?

For someone like Luis, who would have at one time been used to constant attention as the first-born child, the isolation he might have felt as he was relegated to the position of 'just another child,' compounded with the low self-esteem and lack of ability to initiate any form of normal intimacy after his rape, created for him a sense of alienation--one that would later catapult him into life as a shadow of a man, a monster who hunted by night and masqueraded by day, seemingly unimpaired by the scars of his past --using the pseudo personas he'd crafted to lure over 147 boys to grisly deaths.

Researchers in North America and Europe have carefully examined and studied serial killers and their psychological evolution for many years. The investment has supported law enforcement authorities as well as social workers who aim to prevent crimes as well as protect citizens. Colombia has been far less fortunate. With a population of over 41 million, it's far from equipped to deal with the devastating consequences a prolific serial killer leaves on a country's social terrain. They are even less prepared to deal with the horrific fact that, in many ways, it is their own society that failed Luis Garavito, and in so doing allowed him to become the monster he became.

The Hunt: Discovery and Chase

As a country that has been immersed in political and social strife for the past 50 years, Colombia struggles to provide even the most basic security to its citizens. It is this chaos of incessant political unrest that created, in the shadows of every impoverished neighbourhood, the perfect victim pool.

For as crowded as Colombia's streets are, one specific group of people will remain forever unseen--its street children. Colombia's continuous political strife has bred a sub-culture of anonymous children. Garavito carefully selected his prey from the children of low-income households were more vulnerable to the charms of a wandering peddler or a pleasant priest. As the anonymity meant a lower risk of discovery, this was a significant factor in Garavito's crimes going for so long undetected.

April 22nd 1999, was just another day at Los Centauros Park, Villavicencio. Located in Eastern Colombia, the park itself was part of the regular route for an impoverished young boy named Ivan Sabogal, who sold lottery tickets to help fund his schooling.

Ivan's abduction, or rather as it was then noted 'disappearance,' was not discovered until later that evening, when his mother realised he had not returned home by the assigned time. Terrified, Ivan's mother contacted the police and pleaded with them to take on her son's case, hoping to be able to convince them that there was indeed something sinister about Ivan's not coming home that day. In a country like Colombia, as Ivan' mother had little to no power to exert, his abduction could easily have been glossed over, and probably would have been had it not been for the Prosecutor Fernando Aya. Aya had already been investigating the disappearances of 13 other young children over the span of six months. He discovered several mass graves just on the outskirts of Villavicencio and identified a pattern in Ivan's case that was consistent with previous disappearances. Villavicencio was not the only village affected--thousands of miles away, in the heart of Colombia's Coffee District, another set of mothers were desperately trying to apprise the authorities of their missing sons, each hoping against hope that their son would be the one who came home.

The horrors of Garavito's had begun long before that investigation. Years before this, dead children were being discovered all across Colombia in mass graves. One such discovery took place in the quaint little town of Nacederos, where the tortured bodies of fourteen children, ranging from 8 to 14 years old, were unearthed, baffling the Colombian police.

What was even more shocking was the state of the remains. These were not recently deceased bodies. The bodies being unearthed were already decomposed to the point where there was almost no way of individual identification. All that was recoverable at this point were the bones and teeth. Surprisingly, the dental records did initiate a major breakthrough-- none of these children had had work done on their teeth, indicating that they could not afford it, which put them in the same economic sub-group as the missing street children.

Mario Artunduaga, Colombia's most renowned forensic reconstructionist, began working on the bones of the children that were recovered. It was here that the forensic team hit their first major road block. The team soon realised that the diagnostics they were used to working with would not apply to these cases, because the subjects were children as opposed to grown adults. The malleable nature of their bones and the way in which their craniums were constructed called for a major adaptation in process. Artunduaga realised that he would have to create his own methods, and so he did.

Meanwhile, the authorities began to chase down every lead they could. Theories ranged from satanic cults to drug traffickers. Every scrap of evidence was considered and reconsidered. The only thing they could be sure of was that, whatever they were dealing with, they could not afford to miss any clues.

Back in Villavicencio, when Aya was still looking for evidence in his initial investigation, he decided to go and stake out the points of disappearance, hoping that this would allow him to reconstruct the crimes and understand how the abductions took place. Once he arrived at the disappearance points, Aya was confounded. Each one was located in a heavily populated area. How could the abductions have gone unnoticed? Why had the stench of the bodies not been reported? Aya and his team decided to do some ground work in an attempt to figure out exactly how this happened.

Very soon, Aya and his team began to realise how easy it was to miss an abduction in that region. Despite the high population, the area was covered in thick vegetation, and the terrain much too difficult to walk through, making it very difficult for an abduction to have been detected.

In another end of the country, Detective Aldemar Duan, who had previously investigated three similar murders, recognised similarities with other cases all around the country. He cross-referenced the murders against homicides and abductions of a similar nature dating from 1991 to 1998. His hunch became the key to unlocking the mysteries of Garavito's damning pattern.

Forensic scientists were now supplied with evidence such as specific nylon threads, alcohol bottles, and a particular methodology that convinced police that the murders were not the work of a team or organization, that they were dealing with *one* man: a sexual sadist who single-handedly raped and murdered hundreds of Colombia's children.

The Colombian authorities knew that they needed all the help they could get with this case. Colombia had little to no experience managing such cases, so they reached out to their counterparts in the FBI, asking for files on cases similar to the ones they were now investigating.

It was now February of 1999, and yet another mass grave had been unearthed, this time in Palmira, just sixty kilometres south of Nacederos. Carlos Herrera joined the task force. Herrera obtained over thirteen pieces of evidence from this crime scene, one of which was a pair of shoes that would later help investigators identify an important physical characteristic of the murderer. The shoes showed extreme wear towards the ends of the soles, indicating that the shoes were too big for their wearer. Furthermore, the heel of one shoes was nearly worn through, which Herrera concluded indicated a limp or a rotating gait from some sort of injury. The shoes also helped investigators predict the man's height. He would be somewhere between 163 and 167 centimetres tall.

Duran's team decided that if they were to unmask this murderer, they would have to find a way to enter the world he lived in. A handful of Colombia's top detectives went undercover in the country's homeless populace, each in an area the murderer was most likely to target again. The theoretical noose around Garavito's neck tightened further. Finally, the authorities were one step closer.

The Arrest: Unmasking the Man

The 1999 crime scene was largely what broke this case wide open. Herrera pieced together the remnants from the crime scene evidence to create a criminal profile that the murderer would fit into. These tiny little pieces of information would add up to a very specific personality and physical body type, helping the authorities to create a narrow suspect pool.

A pair of charred glasses and a specific brand of alcohol were also recovered from the crime scene. The charring was something that none of the tests could account for, but the lenses did reveal a condition usually specific to two age groups--40 to 45 or 55 to 60. The glasses were also bent at an awkward angle that indicated the wearer probably had widely separated ears.

Aside from age range, height, a preference for a particular brand of alcohol, and two possible distinguishing characteristics, there was still next to no physical evidence that would identify Garavito. As such, the investigators began to focus on behaviour profiling. Various currencies left at the crime scenes hinted that the killer might be moving around Colombia with relative ease, that somehow he was blending in with the crowds of Colombia without raising suspicion.

The investigators decided to look into the victim profile, realising that, given the suspect's probable age, he could have been active much longer than anyone realised and that would mean there might be many more cases than they initially thought.

The authorities pulled over ten years of crime records and allocated roughly 5000 cases to the probable suspect pool. Based on the already known parameters, they removed all with female victims and were left with over 1500 male perpetrators. They then excluded suspects based on height and age and then narrowed the list further by focusing on those who were active in the areas of the already known crime scenes. The final list consisted of 25 names.

Duran's icy determination to capture Garavito had earned him the name 'The Murderous Shadow.' He had become so invested in the case that he flew to Bogata to ascertain more information on the relating case files. It was there that Duran came across another strong lead.

In 1996, there were reports of yet another child who went missing--Renald Delgado, a twelve-year-old boy from the region of Tunja, bordering the north of Bogata. Delgado's case closely matched that of the current victim pool; only, unlike the others, Delgado's case included a suspect. A shopkeeper had reported that the boy had last been seen in the company of a man who was not from the region. That man had been identified and brought in for questioning, only to be released due to a lack of concrete evidence.

This man's name was Luis Alfredo Garavito--a name that appeared on the list of 25 suspects that the investigators had compiled. Duran knew immediately that this was no coincidence. A careful examination of the file revealed other connections. For instance, Garavito's birthplace was registered as Genova, the place where Duran's original three cases had occurred. Furthermore, his place of residence as per his written statement was, Trujillo--the location of yet another mass grave.

The official investigation, however, had taken a different turn. A suspect had been identified in Pereira, one with a limp and in same age range, and he was seen selling honey from the same bottles as those found at the crime scenes. His name was Pedro Pachuga.

On October 1997, two young boys disappeared from a bus station in Pereira, and Pachuga was a top suspect. The boys were later discovered dead. Just days later, another young boy identified Pachuga as an attempted rapist. Sure of their target, the investigators scoured the streets for the man they thought was responsible for the hundreds of bodies strewn across Colombia. Within weeks, the investigators caught and arrested Pedro Pachuga. There was only one catch--Pachuga insisted he was innocent.

During his incarceration, Pachuga continued to plead his innocence, which in itself wasn't unusual, but within weeks the murderer had struck again, this time in Bogata. Four boys murdered with the exact same MO. It became clear that the prosecutors had indeed apprehended the wrong man. The authorities were shaken. The body count was now well past a hundred, and rising. They knew that they needed to take more care in terms of the recovery of evidence, as they could not afford any more mistakes.

The Colombian investigation became a meld of every relevant foreign technique they could reasonably replicate, from the British techniques of evidence recovery with color-coded crime scenes to the Russian and American techniques of forensic facial reconstruction. Soon, four of the victims had been identified by the families--another crucial step in the on-going investigation.

Meanwhile, Duran used the case file on Delgado to track down the address left behind by Luis Alfredo, and in so doing found Ester Garavito Cubillos, a sister of Luis Garavito. Ester was found to have a bag of Garavito's personal items. The bag contained documents, travel mementos, and a collection of journals that revealed intimate details about Garavito's childhood and later life.

Duran's team carefully combed through the documents and found a receipt of money wired to a woman in Pereira, where documents revealed he had been implicated as part of the homicide of a minor by a judicial body in the area. The investigators proceeded to track down the location of the woman, and much to their own surprise they found yet another suitcase of documents, these dating from 1994 to 1997, in her care. The bag contained synthetic fibres, razors, and lubricants, all of which were consistent with what had been uncovered in previous crime scenes. The evidence in Palmira pointed to one further thing--the suspect in question had been burned.

Based on the evidence and the crime scene at Palmira, the investigators came to the conclusion that the suspect would have been wounded and heavily burned as he left in an attempt to distance himself from his latest victim. A man matching his description allegedly sought help at a pharmacy in Pereira, only to disappear right after. This provided yet another physical clue to the suspect's profile. He would have had severe burns along the left side of his body.

By April 22nd, 1999, the search for Ivan Sabogal had intensified. At 11:15 that evening, the police received a call for help from a junkyard employee reporting a boy who claimed to have escaped an attempted rapist. The police responded immediately and, along with Ivan's mother, went to retrieve the boy. She identified the boy instantly. Ivan Sabogal had survived.

Ivan provided a description and then explained how a homeless man had passed by as the predator attempted to assault him, and how that momentary distraction had allowed Ivan to run away. The predator had chased after him and the homeless man, but after being spotted by a young woman as they ran, he had backed off. 'La Bestia' was still out on the streets of Colombia.

The police were prepared to accept the win they had been handed by recovering Ivan Sabogal and were driving him and his mother back to the police station when the unexpected happened. Right there, outside their window, walking along the highway, was a man Ivan identified as his assailant. The man identified himself as Bonofacio Morero Liscado. That name was not on the list of suspects, but with young Ivan's positive identification, the police brought him in for questioning.

Even Bonofacio's arrest was strange, to say the least. The man did not struggle or protest in any way. He was unnervingly calm as he persistently claimed that he was not the man the police were looking for. Nothing he said or did would ever make anyone think that this was a man who had murdered hundreds of children across the Colombian countryside.

Once they reached at the police station, Prosecutor Aya visited the suspect in custody and straightaway noticed the physical similarities between Bonofacio and Luis Alfredo Garavito. He also noticed something the other officers hadn't: on each of the documents that the detainee had signed as Bonofacio, his signature varied.

Ava took his suspicions and a photograph of Bonofacio to a meeting being held with prosecutors from all over the country regarding the murders. It was here that Aya showed Duran and his team the photograph of the man they had in custody. Duran and his team identified him immediately. The man in the picture was Luis Alfredo Garavito. Finally, all the puzzle pieces all fell into place.

The scourge of Colombia was finally behind bars.

Due Process: The Road to Conviction

By the end of this final meeting, authorities were left with little doubt that the man in custody was indeed Luis Alfredo Garavito. He was 42 years old and 167 centimetres tall. He wore glasses and had scars and burns along the left side of his body. He was born in Genova and raised in a dysfunctional family, and had suffered abuse at the hands of parental figures before the age of sixteen--everything fit.

Unfortunately, 'everything' was also completely circumstantial, meaning that without Garavito's confession, the Colombian authorities could prove nothing in a court of law, or at least not enough to build a solid case. The authorities desperately needed to establish concrete links between the crime scene evidence and Garavito himself.

Once again, the investigators started to hunt for evidence to link Garavito to the crimes. Detective Duran, who had now been studying Garavito's profile for years, suggested that there was a possibility that there were more 'memento's' of the victims that Garavito would have saved over the years. They just needed to figure out where they were. It was with this aim in mind that the investigators hunted down Mrs. Umbar Toro, one of Garavito's best friends, and coaxed her into visiting Garavito in jail. The investigators were hoping that Garavito's need to forge a connection would make him open up to this old friend. Sure enough, Garavito confessed to Umbar Toro that there was indeed another bag of documents, which he had left with another inmate's wife.

The contents of this final bag were even more incriminating than those of the first two. The bag contained regional newspaper clippings, paper documents, and even pictures of some of the victims. The bag also contained a scrap of paper with weird markings on it. It was later discovered that the markings were a personal tally of his victims.

Despite all of the evidence, Garavito still refused to confess, and the investigators realised that it was unlikely he ever would. Without a confession, the prosecutors would need an airtight case if they wanted to put Garavito behind bars. Nothing could be left to chance. It was clear that now was the time to establish a concrete link between the evidence collected and Garavito himself. First and foremost, the prosecution would need to establish a DNA link between Garavito and the DNA recovered from the crime scenes. Then there was the matter of the glasses that had been recovered. They needed to be able to determine Garavito's eye condition without tipping him off and thereby giving him the chance to lie about it.

To avoid any disruption on Garavito's part, the entire prison was subjected to an eye exam, and it was during this exam that Garavito's cell was searched for traces of DNA to run against the crime scene samples obtained off the liquor bottles and the bodies. The prescription for the charred glasses came back as a match, and yet the prosecution still didn't think they had enough evidence to seal his fate.

The Colombian authorities decided to use Link, a Dutch software that cross references events, coincidences, and probabilities. They input the software with hotel reports, witness testimonies, and evidence. Link's report placed Garavito at every single crime location at the time of the event, stacking huge weight behind the prosecution's case that Garavito was the only possible perpetrator. They decided that with this software they had enough to secure a conviction, but as a final attempt to make the case as airtight as possible, they decided it was time to take another shot at Luis Garavito himself.

Garavito went through an 8-hour interrogation, with no crack in his demeanour. Garavito remained calm and stable, maintaining the entire time that not only was he innocent, but that all the evidence and witness testimony merely pointed to a flawed investigation. At this point, Lili Naranjo, the head of Garavito's investigation, decided to end the interrogation, recognising that Garavito was far too composed to crack under the pressure they were applying. They knew that they needed a different approach if they were going to destabilise him enough to get a confession. They were going to need someone who knew Garavito better than Garavito himself. Prosecutor Naranjo authorised a private meeting between Garavito and Detective Duran, the only man who knew the cases well enough to go toe-to-toe with Garavito.

What followed would go down forever in the history books as the end of Luis Garavito. Duran decided to approach the only part of Garavito that wasn't capable of staying detached--his fantasy realm. In order to do so, he verbally recounted every one of the murders in intricate detail. He carefully crafted the monologue, taking Garavito back to each of the fantasies he ached to relive. But, the fantasies were not as Garavito remembered them. Duran used explicit detail to build such a vivid mental image of the horrors that Garavito had inflicted, that after 18 hours, Luis Alfredo Garavito, the world's deadliest serial killer, cried out for Detective Duran to stop.

Duran held the murderer in his arms as Garavito, now sobbing, confessed to his crimes by pointing to pictures and explaining in detail what he had done to each of the children and how he had done it. Garavito defended himself by claiming that he had been possessed by 'evil spirits' before each of the kills, theories he attempted to support by referencing his journals. Each of his journals was colour coded blue or red. The blue ones, which he claimed were his own, consisted of Bible verses and other 'pure' thoughts; the red ones contained detailed descriptions of his kills.

In December, Garavito was finally tried and convicted on two counts. The first was for a murder in Tunja, the central province of Boyacá, where 14-year-old Silvino Rodriguez's dismembered and tortured body had been discovered in June 1996. The second count was for the attempted rape of Ivan Sabogal, the 12-year-old boy from western Villavicencio on account of whom he was finally apprehended in April 1999. Garavito had in fact confessed to the murders of over 190 young boys, although experts believe the actual total to be closer to 300. A lack of conclusive evidence, however, prevented Garavito's conviction on the other counts.

The death penalty does not exist in the Colombian legal system, and they had long ago declared that the longest a man could be imprisoned was 60 years. Based on these two counts, Garavito was given this maximum sentence. However, things changed soon after, in 2000, when the Colombian penal code underwent modification, now stating that no individual can be imprisoned for more than 40 years.

Garavito has been described as a 'model prisoner.' He has been studying through his incarceration and has issued a public apology to the people of Colombia. Currently, Garavito is likely to serve a reduced sentence and could be released in 22 years. However, in the face of extreme public pressure, a judicial review of the case has been launched. Garavito could face additional charges for murders that he has not previously confessed to. Such crimes would not fall within the influence of the previous legal process.

True Crime: Victimology and Methodology

The victimology and methodology of a crime are where one will ultimately find answers to the *why*s that crop up during the investigation of a serial killer. Both aspects are crucial in building an offenders profile--a fact that held true in the case of Luis Alfredo Garavito.

Garavito's victims were always male, always ranging from six to sixteen, and generally slim, with brown hair and brown eyes. They were either street children who would not be missed or boys who were impoverished enough to be taken in by the promise of a few coins or sweets. They basically paralleled Garavito himself. Psychologists theorise that for Garavito, the young boys who were from impoverished backgrounds were stand ins for the child Garavito who had suffered a rape or multiple rapes at the hands of his neighbours. Even the age of his victims coincides with the age from which he began to be subjected to abuse, which continued until he finally left home. In Garavito's mind, the children he chose represented his own childhood self.

But it wasn't enough for Garavito to merely abduct a child, or even rape him. There was an entire method to his madness that in the most warped ways made perfect sense. Garavito himself had been raped by neighbours and abused by his father, parental figures, or adults that he trusted. It was this bond of trust that Garavito felt compelled to replicate with his victims. Instead of simply abducting the children, Garavito would build an elaborate ruse, in which he would pose as a monk, a missionary, a humanitarian worker, a handicapped old man, or even at times a harmless street peddler. In each instance, Garavito spent time talking to his victims, carefully using his assumed persona to build trust between himself and the child. This bond that he created was, in a way, a balm to his soul. It was how he explained away his mistake in trusting his neighbours. Surely, if so many boys did the same, it wasn't really his 'fault' that he had been victimised the way he had.

But it wasn't just the victim profiles that defined Garavito's crimes. Rather, his crimes followed a strict systematic procedure, one that was indicative of his sadistic and sociopathic nature. Garavito would first rape and then torture his victims. It is worth noting that the torture was a part of his methodology rather than a part of the sexual act itself. It was not important for him to torture the boys. Rather, the torture came as an after thought, usually followed by slitting their throats and dismembering their corpses--the final act of degradation. An act that points to the reconstruction of his own childhood trauma, only amplified. He consistently used screwdrivers or knives to commit these acts.

Recently, Luis Garavito, or *La Bestia*, as he is better known, has expressed an intention to start a political career once he is released. He has also gone on record to state his intention to work with abused children as part of this political career. The disturbing fact is that, with the Colombian legal system being what it is, it is entirely possible that this erstwhile mass murderer, who once littered the Colombian landscape with his kills, will leave his maximum security holding cell in just a few short years to do just that.

Pedro Alonzo Lopez: 'The Monster of the Andes'

The Making of a Monster

It has been said that if evil had a face, it would be that of Pedro Lopez. This leads one to ask, what caused this seemingly normal man to become the monster that history remembers him as?

Lopez was a man who had undoubtedly been dealt a cruel hand by fate. Born to a prostitute in Tolima, the seventh of thirteen children, Pedro had grown up hiding behind the ragged curtains of his ramshackle home as he watched his mother be sexually objectified by different men every day. It was a life where nothing was sacred, which is perhaps what lead eight-year-old Pedro to do the unthinkable and sexually molest his own sister, an act that lead to his being kicked out his dank, horror-filled childhood home at a tender age.

Alone and terrified, on a cold night in 1957, eight-year-old Pedro Alonzo Lopez found himself expelled from his own home, ordered to never return. It was in that moment that Lopez realised how expendable he was. His victimisation is likely to have intensified during this phase of his life (a matter further explored in Chapter Four). Exiled for sexually assaulting his own sister, Pedro walked the dark streets of Tolmia, trying desperately to come to terms with the edict handed down by his mother. The first time he went home, refusing to stay away, his access was denied. The next time he tried, his mother not only prevented him from re-joining the family but went a step further and dropped him off at the city border with no food, no shelter, no support, and no options. Pedro was at his most vulnerable, but his luck was about to change (for a brief moment). A ray of hope came walking by in the form of an older man who found Pedro wandering around the streets. The man stopped, spoke to him, and finally decided to help him.

For Pedro, this man was his shot at doing things over, and more importantly doing things right. This man promised food and shelter and was offering Pedro a chance at absolution. Or so he thought.

The older man who took Pedro Alonzo Lopez off the Tolima streets in 1957 with the promise of food and shelter was unfortunately not a Good Samaritan hoping to help a vulnerable child. He was a predator. That night, eight-year-old Pedro Lopez was not taken home to a plush bed and warm food. He was taken instead to an abandoned building where cold grasping hands tore the clothes off his back and raped him repeatedly, only to finally toss him out onto the filthy Colombian streets once again.

This betrayal of faith, so soon after he'd lost his only sense of stability, ruined Pedro's trust in humanity in the most basic ways, but most of all it destroyed his trust in adults. Pedro Lopez soon began to go to unnatural lengths to avoid contact with any adult. At the peak of his trauma, young Pedro hid out in dark alleyways or deserted buildings on the mean streets of Tolima, leaving his carefully scouted sanctuaries only to scavenge for food in the nearby bins and trash fills--a pitiful existence that became all Pedro knew for over a year.

Pedro's mother, in her attempt to protect her daughter against further sexual trauma, had sentenced Pedro to a lifetime of trauma, one that he would never truly overcome.

The following year, Pedro finally gathered enough courage to travel across the country to a small town named Bogata, coincidentally a town where Luis Garavito had also been active. Once he arrived in Bogata,

Pedro went back to scavenging and begging for food. It seemed he had to some degree been able to overcome his aversion towards adults, and it was thus that he met yet another set of adults who would play a life-changing role in his life. An elderly American couple was so heartbroken at the sight of the young child scavenging for food that they offered to take him home. Realising that, realistically, he had next to no other options, Pedro took the leap of faith and went with them.

It seems evident that this decision would further influence Pedro into becoming the 'Monster of the Andes'. This was not directly down to the elderly couple, as they were nothing but kind to Pedro, providing him food and board and enrolling him in a school for orphans. In fact, it was just as his life began to regain a sense of normality that Pedro Alonzo Lopez was reminded that *he* would never be lucky enough to be saved.

At 12 years old, Pedro Lopez was sexually molested yet again, this time by a male teacher at the school he had been enrolled in. This was the last straw. Pedro Lopez was tired of being the victim.

He began to feel the anger grow inside of him, and using all his previous fears to channel courage and aggression, Pedro carefully planned the theft of a large sum of money from the school's office then fled back to the streets of Colombia that he now considered his only safe haven.

It was now 1963, and with the civil war drawing to a close, businesses were opening up once again. Unfortunately for Pedro, he was neither trained nor educated well enough to be able to take advantage of this growing economy. He instead resorted to begging for food once again for almost six years, eventually turning to petty theft for survival.

Pedro's initial foray into theft was probably an early indicator of how he had lost any respect for the concepts of right and wrong. He soon shifted to car theft as a teen and became impressively adept at it. Not only was he well paid for his services, but also, for the first time in his life, he was sought after. For someone like Pedro, who had never fit in anywhere, such valuation was likely highly comforting and addictive.

Like everything else in his life, however, this too fell apart. At eighteen, Pedro was arrested for car theft and sentenced to seven years in jail. Two days in, Pedro was gang raped by four adult inmates. He furiously swore to himself that never again would he allow his abusers to get away unscathed. Pedro spent the next two weeks fashioning a crude knife from prison utensils, then hunted down his four attackers and stabbed them to death.

Much like Luis Garavito, Pedro Lopez's childhood does in many ways explain how he became all that he became. The detached, vicious, and morally corrupt madman who roamed the length of the Andes was manufactured by a Colombian society that continuously failed him. This is not to say that his misfortune exonerates him or justifies anything he did, but it does explain many of his actions and reactions.

What it doesn't explain, however, is Pedro's sadistic enjoyment of not just the act but the web of manipulation that he weaved around his victims, and for that we must step into the mind of the man himself.

The State vs Lopez: The Discovery and Chase

Unlike most other serial killers, Pedro's story actually begins from when he was in jail. An angst-filled teenager with revenge on his mind, Pedro Lopez murdered four men within the first month of his imprisonment. Surprisingly, Pedro was not convicted for the murders. The prison authorities, who had been aware of the four men and their prior assault on the eighteen-year-old, decided to list Pedro's act as one of self-defence, allowing him to get off with a mere two years added to his previous sentence. Nine years later, in 1978, Pedro Alonzo Lopez was released from prison.

Now twenty-seven years old, Pedro Lopez was no longer the young man who had once scavenged for food. His past experiences, in addition to having spent his formative years in prison, made Pedro veer toward an extremely anti-social personality. Pedro later claimed that, because of his mother's abuse and the way he had come to view adults, he found it difficult to even hold a conversation with an adult female. He needed to find an alternative, and so he did.

Pedro Lopez began to travel widely through Peru soon after his release from prison. He later admitted that during this time he stalked and murdered at least a hundred young girls from various native tribes across the region. He began to realise that younger females were more susceptible to his meagre charms and therein found the solution to his difficulty with women.

Pedro's new solution was put to a halt when he was captured in Northern Peru by a native tribe known as the Ayachucos. At the time, Pedro had been attempting to abduct a nine-year-old tribal girl.

Infuriated, the tribe stripped Lopez bare and flayed him for hours before finally deciding to bury him alive. Once again, however, an American missionary intervened. The lady in question convinced the tribe that Lopez ought to be handed over to the appropriate authorities, and that since she was on her way to the town square, she could easily drop him off at the nearest police station. The tribe reluctantly agreed and tied Pedro up to the back of her truck.

The missionary delivered Lopez to the local authorities. However, because of the cultural divide, the Peruvian police were unwilling to 'waste' their time by investigating 'petty' complaints lodged by natives. Instead, Peruvian authorities released the rapist and serial killer into Ecuador, where the second phase of Lopez's murder spree commenced.

Upon regaining his freedom, Lopez began to do the exact same thing he had done when he was released from prison. He travelled extensively, lured, young women in, and murdered them. The majority of this happened in Colombia. The authorities began to notice an increase in the number of missing people on their reports. Because of their ages, the authorities initially thought that the children were runaways, but soon it became clear there was a pattern evolving. All the victims were young, attractive females. The number of disappearances and the similarities of the cases led authorities to suspect a sex slave or prostitution ring was involved. Not in their wildest dreams did they imagine that the hundreds of missing girls were the work of one single person.

Bodies began to appear in other places. Initially, since there were only one or two bodies at a time, the authorities didn't know whether to associate them with the mass disappearances. Dr Rothman Rios, who was the medical examiner at the time, explained that the bodies themselves did not indicate any significant links. There was little to no evidence to suggest who was behind the murders, and no witnesses. It began to seem like whoever was responsible had managed to commit the perfect crimes.

In March 1980, a flash flood near Ambato, Ecuador, unearthed four bodies. All four were female. All four had been sadistically tortured. The idea that these four women were just victims of random murders, when the country was besieged by an increase in missing women, was hard to argue. The authorities were forced to reconsider. There was clearly more to these disappearances than slavery or prostitution rings.

The discovery of the four bodies from the flood and the constant disappearance of young girls put the entire country on edge. The fact that the police had no leads made the entire population paranoid. Mothers with young daughters realised that the murderer could literally be anyone, as could the victims. It was this countrywide wariness that would lead to the capture of Pedro Lopez.

Just days after the flash flood unearthed the bodies of four victims, Pedro Lopez was to stalk his last victim. It was early morning, and Carlina Ramon Poveda, a vendor at the local market, was setting up her stall with her young daughter in tow. Lopez had entered the market posing as a peddler who was selling chains, padlocks, and other similar wares. He continued selling all day until late in the afternoon, when he finally approached Carlina's food stall and pretended to look into her pots and pans to see what she was cooking. Meanwhile, the stranger began to sneak looks at Carlina's eleven-year-old daughter, Maria. Maria became flustered by the man's attentions and went to her mother. She told her the man had been looking at her and beckoning to her.

Realizing that this abduction was not going to be as easy as he'd previously thought, Pedro Lopez quietly slipped out of the market. However, by then Maria had already alerted her mother, who realised that there was a strong possibility that this was the man the entire country was looking for. Within minutes, Carlina gathered some of her vendor friends and chased down the unknown man, who had just made his way to the main entrance.

The authorities were summoned immediately. Pedro Lopez, when they found him, was babbling incoherently, so much so that the authorities initially presumed they had captured a madman--failing to realise that the man they now held in custody and were driving to local police headquarters was the Monster of the Andes.

The Unveiling of a Madman

Once he had been taken to police headquarters, Lopez adopted a silent pout, which, much to the dismay of the officers in charge, he maintained throughout the entire questioning procedure. It wasn't that Lopez was scared or frustrated in the way Luis Garavito had been. It was more like he was bored and was enjoying flustering the authorities. Realising that the regular scare tactics would not work on this particular suspect, the authorities decided to use a very different approach. At this point, the police did not suspect Lopez to be guilty of anything more than the murders of the children whose bodies had been uncovered weeks before in the flash flood.

An officer on duty suggested that one of them dress up as the local priest and attempt to win over the man's confidence. Ultimately, "Pastor Cordoba Gudina," who was the Captain at the time, entered Lopez's cell and sat with him through the night. Soon enough, the Padre began to win over Lopez's confidence by regaling him with tales of crimes he professed to have committed as a rapist. Lopez began to contribute to the conversation the young Padre had initiated. Each story was more gruesome than the prior, each revealing such bone-chilling acts of inhuman degradation of the victim that at one point even the seasoned officer could no longer sit there listening to them. The detective, who remained undercover for nearly an entire month, was stunned.

Pedro Lopez had by then gleefully informed the undercover Padre that he had been travelling through Ecuador, Peru, and Colombia for the past three years, and by his own count had raped and killed over three hundred young girls--a claim that, if proven to be true, would rank him as one of the most prolific serial killers in the world.

By the next morning, authorities had been able to gather enough evidence to finally confront Lopez with his crimes. This time Lopez finally spoke up. Pedro Lopez o, as he came to be known, The Monster of the Andes, claimed proudly that he had raped and murdered over one hundred and ten young girls in Ecuador, at least a hundred in Peru, and, as he put it 'many more than a hundred' in Colombia, going on to state that he only really enjoyed the girls in Ecuador, claiming their trusting nature made them more 'appealing,' as opposed to the stranger-wary little girls back in Colombia.

In his own words, "I like the girls in Ecuador. They are more gentle and trusting, more innocent. They are not as suspicious of strangers as Colombian girls."

It was at this point that the police began to reach out to their neighbouring countries to see if there ware any cases to corroborate his claims. It made no sense that a serial killer could have been active in three countries and yet remain entirely undetected by the authorities in all of them.

Lopez was relishing this new-found attention. He started to talk about his own childhood and the many ways in which society had failed him. Each reference to his own tragic past he made more apathetically, as he logically reasoned how he had become the monster he was claiming to be. At one point, he specifically pinpointed the moment he decided to become a serial killer. "I lost my innocence at age eight, so I decided to do the same to as many young girls as I could."

Still, the police could not make sense of the sheer number of murders Lopez was confessing to, and when both Colombian and Peruvian Authorities failed to substantiate his claims, Lopez began to realise that the authorities didn't quite believe him. So, Lopez did the only thing a narcissistic psychopath such as himself could do: he offered to take them to the bodies.

The Law of the Land: Conviction and Beyond

One would think that with half a dozen dead bodies and a confirmed confession, Pedro Lopez would be behind bars without question. That was not, however, how Pedro Lopez's case was to go. Once he'd provided his initial confession, Pedro realises that the local authorities doubted the veracity of his claims. So, he offered to take them out to the gravesites to prove to the truth of his proud claims.

Initially hesitant, the local police finally decided to allow Lopez to guide them to the gravesites, which he claimed were scattered all over the country. Over the span of six weeks, Lopez led the police across eleven Ecuadorian provinces, at each revealing yet another gruesome collection of bodies. For his own safety, the police required Lopez to dress as a police officer when he accompanied them out to the gravesites. There was a guard placed on either side of him, both for his protection and to thwart any attempt at escape.

The first gravesite was just on the border of Ambato. He described the girl as a newspaper seller who he had abducted, raped, and then murdered just ten months earlier. He told them he'd buried her under a specific bridge in the locality. To their surprise, the police found a complete skeleton, as described, at the base of the bridge. The medical examiner was unable to determine any specifics of the crime from the body, other than a corroded arm and leg, evidence of the torture he'd inflicted on the young child. However, the police soon gained the clarity they sought after one of the victim's family members was brought to the site. They recognised the clothes hanging off the bones of the skeleton and confirmed what Lopez had told the police. The bones belonged to a young girl named Ortensia Garces Lozada.

Lopez's claims were shockingly accurate, and as the police moved on to the next location, they found more and more bodies. The police shared some blame for these horrendous atrocities. The disappearances had begun long before the identity and capture of Lopez, but investigations never really amounted to anything. Even in the case of Ortensia, the police had refused to investigate the case, insisting that it merely an incident of a runaway child. The locals claim that such bias was due to the class divide. For the most part, Lopez's victims had been from impoverished families, which was why they would fall for his lures of money so easily. Ortensia, for instance, had been lured away by a mere ten dollars.

Roughly two months after Ortensia, that Lopez chose the wrong victim--nine year old Evanova Jacome. As the daughter of a successful baker, Evanova's disappearance was responded to in ways that none of the other girls' had been. Immediately, there was media coverage and flyers were distributed all across Ecuador, with the police working day and night to find her. It was this burst of media attention that had triggered the wave of suspicion back in April. Evanova's body, displaying evidence of both rape and mutilation, was eventually found on an abandoned farm, .

Pedro Lopez's trip down memory lane would go on for over fifty-three gravesites. At each gravesite, Lopez would display the exact same amount of amusement and satisfaction, as if each grave marked a victory in his name. His pride was sickening, and yet the police had little choice but to follow him around and encourage him to take them to the next site. They desperately needed the information that only Lopez himself could give them. So, they continued to supply him with cigarettes and alcohol.

Lopez began to develop a friendship with the captain he had initially confessed to. In fact, at one point, Pedro began to refer to the captain as 'Father,' an impulse the police later attributed to his lack of a fatherly figure in his own life.

Finally, when the police began to realise that Lopez was leading them to already compromised gravesites (possibly from wild animals or floods), they decided to bring him back to the police headquarters, where he was charged with fifty-seven counts of murder--for the fifty-three gravesites and four corpses discovered in the floods. It was Lopez's own detailed confessions, however, that lead to him being charged with one hundred and ten murders. Victor Lascano, at that time governor of the Ambato jail, told reporters that, in his personal opinion, the tally of three hundred girls that Lopez claimed to have murdered was likely a low estimate.

Pedro Lopez openly confessed to over three hundred murders, calling himself 'worse than an animal,' and yet showed no sign of regret in his actions or words. His voice was calm, steady, and unemotional. Lopez had been caught in Ecuador, a country that had become a favourite hunting grounds for serial killers due to the sentencing laws. No matter the nature or number of murders the maximum conviction was sixteen years. By confessing to all of his crimes, Lopez was ensuring he could not be tried again in that same jurisdiction for the crimes he was confessing to--a judicial practice known as 'double jeopardy.' Ecuadorian law also prohibits consecutive sentencing, meaning he could only be sentenced to sixteen years total rather than sixteen years per murder. He was convicted nine months after his arrest, by Judge Jose Roberto, in a southern town in Ambato, close to where he was first apprehended.

This mockery of a sentence was of no solace to the families who had lost their girls. Pedro Lopez, by his calculations, would be spending only seventeen days in jail per murder he'd confessed to. Outraged, the families demanded a reform of the prison laws, but the Prison Minister, Pablo Faguero, responded with, "Yes, it does sound strange, but that is our law."

Fourteen years after his sentencing, on August 31st 1994, Pedro Alonzo Lopez walked free. His behaviour in jail had been so exemplary that the 'Monster of the Andes' had had his sentence reduced by two years. However, the Ecuadorian authorities detained him an hour after his release. Lopez discovered that the superintendent of the province had ordered him back into custody, claiming that he was an illegal immigrant who did not have proper documentation. The only logical step therefore was to hand him over to the Colombian authorities. The hope was that, once on Colombian soil, Pedro Lopez would be forced to face the harsher laws of his country of origin.

The very next day, Lopez was handed over to Colombian authorities at the Rumichaca Bridge, which connects Ecuador and Colombia. After more than two decades, Pedro Alonzo Lopez was home. On arrival, Lopez was picked up by Colombian National Security and was immediately processed and sent to Tolima for prosecution. In December 1979, he had travelled to El Espinal, a small town in Tolima.

Within months, a ten-year-old girl by the name of Flore Sanchez had disappeared. Sanchez's body had later been found and identified by her mother. The pattern and methodology of this twenty-year-old murder fit Lopez's previous methodology perfectly. Along with the evidence gathered by the police, Colombian authorities had everything they needed to secure another conviction.

Yet, by another stroke of luck, Lopez once again found himself saved. In 1995, he was declared mentally incompetent on grounds of insanity and incarcerated in the psychiatric wing of a prison in Bogata. Three years later, Lopez was declared sane on evaluation by the prison psychiatrist. He was then released on the condition that he attend monthly sessions with a judge and continue to receive psychiatric treatment--both of which requirements Lopez would later forgo.

Upon his release, Lopez decided to go back to his roots and visit his mother, Benilda, for the first time in nineteen years. He slipped back into his terrifyingly cruel persona, taunting his impoverished mother by selling her belongings before her very eyes. Pedro kept the meagre earnings from the sale and walked back into the countryside he had once littered with the bodies of little girls never to be seen again.

The Psychology of a Psychopath

The Monster of the Andes' has provided one interview in his lifetime--to a Mr. Ron Laytner of Edit International. This one interview, in combination with his confession and the evidence obtained at the gravesites, has allowed us to piece together what went on in the mind of Pedro Lopez--the man and the murderer.

Investigators have been trying to understand the psychology behind one of South America's most deadly men so that they can ascertain both his victimology and methodology. After all, with Lopez on the loose, it might only be a matter of time before the Monster strikes again.

Victimology and Modus Operandi

For a man whose victim count is in the hundreds, it is remarkable how consistent he has always been with his victim choices. As most profilers will tell you, victim profiling is still a relatively new mode of investigation. However, it offers great value to authorities both by helping to predict prospective targets and identify specific events in the serial killer's own life that can point to the perpetrator.

In the case of Pedro Alonzo Lopez, all of the victims were little girls, aged from eight to twelve. As discussed earlier, this was the same age that Pedro was first molested. It's also the same age he was forced to leave his house for molesting his sister. When asked in his interview why he only ever chose young victims Pedro stated, "It's like eating chicken. Why eat old chicken when you can have young chicken?"

His was intended to elicit shock and repulsion. A mass murderer who shamelessly confesses to his crimes does not have a lot to hide.

Remember that Lopez revelled in the horror he inflicted. Theories suggest that this was a reflection of his fear of adults as well as his revulsion for adult females.

FBI profiler Robert Ressler once famously pointed out that, especially in cases like Lopez's, a serial killer will often have an obsession of sorts with their mother, one that would manifest in a love-hate relationship. In cases of mothers who presented with sexualised lives, this obsession would manifest with an edge to it--meaning his selection of young women was indicative of his complex relationship with his mother as well as the abuse he suffered at an early age at the hand of sexual predators. In Lopez's warped mind, he viewed the innocence of the girls, as well as their age, as a reflection of his own naiveté, which he perhaps was attempting to purge from the girls.

Some profilers have theorised that, in his mind, Lopez actually considered himself to be helping the girls, indicated by the way he would refer to them as his 'dolls.' They posit that his notion of being their 'saviour'--despite his torture, rape, and murder routine--could be a reflection his feelings about poverty and life as a victim of sexual abuse. It could be that he saw death as a gift, and that in his eyes he was giving them the release none of his abusers had been 'kind' enough to provide him.

Even Lopez's method of luring the girls was reflective of his own abusive past. Lopez would bait them by offering sweets or money, material lures similar to those offered to eight-year-old Lopez when roamed the streets of Tolima by himself. The way he had responded to the lures must have been something he regretted and berated himself for as a child and as an adult. Watching little girls the same age make the same mistake he had was likely cathartic for Lopez--it absolved him. What he had done to 'contribute' to his abuse was a mistake hundreds of children would make. This also explains why he preferred the Ecuadorian girls to the Colombian girls. The girls he hunted in Colombia were much more wary--a reminder of what he had not been. Their suspicion spoiled Pedro's satisfaction in the kills.

The abuse Lopez endured was a catalyst for the 'Monster,' this viciousness that the acts of rape and torture reflected.

Pedro Alonzo Lopez may have killed over three hundred young girls, and he remembered every one of them. At no point did they blur into each other. These murders were not done in an attempt to purge something from his memory. In fact, it was more as if they were keeping a memory alive--allowing him to live it again and again. Acts born not of a compulsion he was forced to satisfy, but rather the indulgence of a luxury.

How do we know?

Look at how Lopez committed the crimes. His signature move throughout the murders was strangulation. He stated that the moment of the kill was the most precious--the moment he watched her life force slowly drain from her body. Of his victims, three had been strangled so ferociously that their eyes popped out of their sockets. Lopez tried to explain this fetish by likening it to the 'moment of truth' in bullfights, as if he were the spectator watching either the bull or the matador realised he is facing certain death. Strangulation was a very risky method. It left behind evidence, and it was slow. With Lopez's level of intelligence, something must have compensated for those drawbacks. Identifying that reward is the key to understanding what drove him.

Like most sexual sadists, Lopez felt that his ability to control the moment of death gave him power. He had lacked that sense of control his entire life. He began as a street kid with no way to ever amount to anything more than just that. As a man, the Monster of the Andes was not some powerless street rat who could be used and abused at will. He was powerful, a force to be reckoned with. Lopez derived pleasure from controlled acts of violence. That's what sets him apart from Garavito, for whom killing was just an afterthought.

That's also what makes him so dangerous, because it suggests that Pedro Lopez--now a free man--is far from done.

Some people claim they've seen Pedro Lopez somewhere in the mountain ranges he once haunted, while some claim that he was murdered by the kin of the families he ripped apart--but the truth is, no one really knows. It is this uncertainty that causes the people of the Andes to look over their shoulders as they walk their daughters to the fish market, or warn them never to talk to strangers when they send them on an errand. After all, it was the Monster of the Andes himself who said, with calm prophetic intent, "Someday, when I am released, I will feel that moment again. I will be happy to kill again. It is my mission."

Daniel Camargo Barbosa: 'The Sadist of El Charquito'

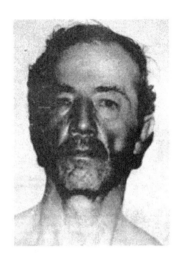

The Creation of Camargo

Historically, the term 'genius' has usually been used to denote superior intellect. With intellect being the measure of a person's ability to process and deal with information, the term genius has normally held positive connotations, reserved for intellectuals whose application of that intellect was deserving of recognition.

A world in which history defines genius by pure intellect would also be a world in which mass-murdering psychopaths such as Daniel Camargo Barbosa would be referred to as 'genius.'

Shocked?

Born with an IQ of over 160, Daniel Camargo Barbosa's story is very different from that of Luis Garavito or Pedro Lopez, and there is a specific set of reasons to illustrate why.

For years there has been a revolving theory amongst criminal psychologists that suggests that certain serial killers are not born psychopaths. People who are born psychopaths begin to display signs of sociopathic behaviour-- such as being aloof, small scale sadistic tendencies, or even sexualised sadism--early on. A specific trigger launches them down the murderous path they become notorious for. There is, however, another type of serial killer--men and women who are not born with prominent psychopathic tendencies, with no manifestations of sociopathic tendencies in early childhood. They generally display a high level of intelligence, which makes them a malicious and particularly scary breed. Daniel Camargo Barbosa was one of these types.

Daniel Barbosa's body count, even at its maximum estimation, does not hold a candle to Garavito's. His methodology, so far as gruesomeness is concerned, is nothing compared to the brutality of Pedro Lopez's. Neither of these factors is what makes Daniel Camargo's story so chilling. His reputation stems from the destruction he wrought wherever he went. He was a master manipulator, capable of using mere words to convince a young woman to bring him virgin sacrifices and even persuade hardened prison guards to help him escape a prison as impregnable as Gorgona Island. He was, in many ways, the real-life manifestation of Sir Arthur Conan Doyle's Moriarty--a fact as unsettling as it is fascinating.

Camargo's Early Childhood

Born on the 22nd of January, 1930, in the quaint little town of Anolaima, Cundinamarca, Daniel Camargo's early childhood was the very embodiment of a picturesque Colombian upbringing. Camargo was born to Teresa Briceno just as Colombia began to drag itself up from the ditches of the aftermath of its civil war and into a new relative peace, which ushered in its wake Enrique Olaya Herrera's rise to power. Until this point, Daniel was by all accounts a happy, cheerful child--until tragedy struck. When he was two years old, Daniel and his half sister Cecilia lost their mother. Their widowed father, like many men of those regions, chose to remarry within the space of a few months--a move that would play a critical role in Camargo's story.

Daniel's father had always been an emotionally distant man. This distance gave rise to hostility on Daniel's part when it became evident that his father had little patience or time for young Daniel, therefore leaving him vulnerable to his abusive teenage bride, Dioselina Fernandez.

Camargo's relationship with his stepmother was a significant contributor to his development--both his sadism and his resentment for women. Reports indicate that while his stepmother shared an amiable relationship with his half-sister Cecilia, Dioselina Fernandez displayed psychopathic tendencies such as sadistic physical and psychological abuse towards young Daniel. Camargo spoke at length about his stepmother during interrogation. His statements illustrate her as being extremely abusive, both mentally and physically.

In one interview in particular, Camargo described his stepmother forcing him to take off his pants and then mercilessly beating him with a cattle whip. In another, he talked about how she would force him to wear dresses and go out in public so that he could be 'publically shamed.' In some reports, neighbours said that it was Camargo's behaviour that triggered the need for punishments. Psychologists claim that this tendency to overlook abusive behaviour is a result of the 'mask of sanity' worn by the abuser. It's likely Daniel's stepmother presented his behaviour to the outside world in such a way as to justify her actions.

It is a well-documented fact that a combination of psychological and physical abuse will scar a child's psyche. Daniel was eventually forced to adopt a defence system to protect himself from the inhumane treatment he had suffered at the hands of his father's new spouse. Camargo was a child of extraordinary intellect, so it was only natural that he perceived his circumstance as a problem in need of a solution. His solution was to become a master manipulator. He realised early on that telling the truth was not getting him anywhere with his dysfunctional family, so young Daniel resorted to half-truths, manipulation, and outright deceit to 'save' himself. Many years later, these same techniques would serve him to simply get what he wanted.

Adulthood and Beyond

As an adult, Daniel applied his persuasive skills in the world of sales. He became a door-to-door salesman for brands such as General Electric, Olympic and Blot Man. During this time, Daniel met and married his first wife, Alcira Castillo in the year 1957. As a newly married man, Daniel realised that his meagre income as a salesman was not enough to maintain a proper homestead. It was at this point that Daniel first began to consider alternative income sources, both legal and illegal. In 1958, Camargo was charged with the robbery of a tailoring shop. This event was to prove extremely significant to the evolution of Camargo's felonious persona, not because he was arrested, but because mere hours after his arrest, Daniel Camargo walked out of the jail a free man.

The idea of an arrested felon walking out of a police station is reminiscent of something out of a Hollywood movie. In his own words, Camargo describes the event by saying, "The moment I entered the jail, the officers were out. I walked in, grabbed an abandoned folder off a desk, tucked it under my arm, and simply walked off into the street."

Camargo walked out of the police station and back home, to the arms of his wife and their Eduardo Santos home in Southern Bogota, then went back to work. For a while, everything seemed perfect. But perfection was not something that Camargo's life would hold on to for very long, and things changed very quickly just four years later.

On one particular day in 1962, Camargo had spent all day going door to door with a sales catalogue for mixers and other home appliances when a torrential downpour hit the city streets. Exhausted and now drenched, Camargo decided to call it a day and go home early. Little did he know the absolute betrayal he would find when he got home. While Camargo was out walking the streets of Bogota trying to provide for himself and his wife, his spouse had spent her days having an affair with another man.

Camargo did not immediately react to his wife's betrayal. Instead, he waited outside for hours for the man to leave. Once he had, Camargo silently retrieved his belongings and left to go back to his childhood home. He went back to his job as a door-to-door salesman and continued his life in the absence of his wife. One year later, he met the woman who would help him become the 'Sadist of Charquito.'

Before we get into the details of Camargo's relationship with this mysterious woman, it is important to understand that since his wife's betrayal, Camargo began to develop an unhealthy obsession for purity. This obsession would feed his *modus operandi* as well as his psychological reasoning for the brutal rapes and murders he is notorious for.

In 1963, when Camargo met Esperanza, she was a drugstore attendant at the Granada City Centre. While Esperanza was only a year younger than Camargo, she was submissive by nature. This allowed Camargo take on the role of a dominant, controlling partner. These traits came into full force when Camargo realised, during an intimate moment, that Esperanza was not a virgin. This conflict between his ideals of purity and his affection for Esperanza acted as Camargo's trigger.

Inside the Mind of a Murderer

The young, submissive Esperanza was the perfect foil for Daniel Camargo's domineering and manipulative self. Having found himself at the mercy of abusive and unfaithful women for years, Daniel found that he had now shifted into a role of a dominance--and what better way to maintain this position of superiority than by ensuring his submissive Esperanza was reminded daily of how shameful her lack of virginity was. At one point, Camargo persuaded Esperanza that since she failed to preserve her own virginity for him, she now owed it to him to bring him virgin sacrifices in her stead. And so began a string of rape cases that would terrorise the city of Granada.

Initially, Esperanza provided her own two younger sisters to Camargo as sacrifices. The couple had had them over for dinner, and Esperanza laced their food with sedatives that she obtained from her workplace. Once they were unconscious, she left them alone with Camargo for hours. Far from being enough, these rapes only served to whet Camargo's newly found appetite for sadism. Knowing that he could use Esperanza's desperation to make up for her lack of virginity to control her, Camargo enticed her with promises of marriage while simultaneously threatening to leave her. All she had to do to ensure he didn't was continue to bring him virgins.

Esperanza did exactly as Camargo instructed. It wasn't long before a routine was established. She would dress in the blue uniform common to Granada's major supermarket chains, enter the stores, and wait with Camargo for the perfect girl. The girls were all young, no older than ten to fourteen years, and were also attractive. Once he'd selected his target, Camargo would approach the girls as they left the shop and accuse them of theft. When the girls began to deny the theft and get panicky, Esperanza would come in and tell them not to worry, and that if they accompanied her to the manager's office they would be able to persuade the manager not to call the police.

Terrified, the young girls would follow the sadistic couple. Half-way to the 'manager's office,' they would take a detour at a coffee shop, where Camargo would offer the girls a pill to take the edge off. The pills were actually Sodium Seconal--sleeping pills. After they dosed their victims, the couple would carry them off on public transport, under the guise of being a family, to Camargo's home, where Esperanza would give them a stronger dose of sedatives and then leave them to be violated all night.

In a macabre twist, the couple would then drop the children off in front of their homes in the early hours of the morning. They continued their reign of terror for over a year.

The media began to refer to the mysterious woman who abducted these women as 'The Lady in Blue,' since the presence of a woman in blue was the only connection they could derive from the abductions. But it wasn't until twelve-year-old Monica was abducted that the rest of the gruesome details came to light.

Monica had gone to the downtown stores in Bogata with her aunt to buy a pencil at around 6pm and was about to leave the store when a man approached her and accused her of stealing a purse. Monica denied having stolen anything, but the man continued to insist she had, and it was at this moment that 'The Lady in Blue' approached them and suggested that they go resolve this issue at the manager's office. On the way there, the couple paused briefly at a coffee shop, where Monica was offered a pill to calm her down. Monica's next recollection was standing in front of her house knowing that she'd been raped.

The next day, Monica went to the police and provided them her statement, which would later lead to the capture of Daniel Camargo and his accomplice. The police began to deploy undercover officers all around Bogata's downtown shopping areas, as they suspected the couple employed the same routine every time. All they had to do was carefully survey the shops for a man fitting Camargo's description.

Just months later, in 1964, a man fitting the rapist's description was spotted and approached by undercover officers who asked him to identify himself. Knowing that he was already a fugitive from the law, Camargo immediately attempted to flee the scene. The officer in pursuit prevented his escape by shooting him twice in the leg from behind.

The news of the rapist's arrest spread quickly. Terrified, Esperanza immediately surrendered to the authorities and even provided a detailed account of the crimes, claiming that Camargo had forced her to take part. Her reports were enough to convict Camargo for up to six years.

On the 10th of April, 1964, Daniel Camargo Barbosa was convicted and sentenced to three years in prison. Camargo was so grateful for the lenient sentence that he supposedly swore to repent and steer away from a life of crime. However, just days before his final sentencing, his case was handed over to a new judge who instead sentenced him to eight years in Bogata's Modelo Prison. Camargo claims that it was this last minute change in sentencing that provoked him to recant his pledge, leading him instead to count down the days until his release and return to crime.

The Evolution of a Murderer

During his time in prison, Camargo was known to read voraciously, a habit he continued after his release. He also kept a journal documenting most of his actions after his release. It's this journal that helps us understand most of what really happened to Camargo, through his own words. Outside of the journal, Camargo, unlike the two other serial killers discussed in this book, remained tight-lipped about his killing sprees.

Camargo's evolution was gradual, almost as if it came in phases: his initial phase in Brazil was followed by the murders in Barranquilla, Colombia, and then a final phase in Ecuador.

Phase One

Right after Camargo's release, a strange series of events befell Colombia. Young women from thirteen to twenty-two years old began to disappear, eventually turning up brutally raped and strangled in mass graves. The way the victims were selected and the manner in which they were left strangled prompted locals to believe that there was a 'vampire' preying on the women of the capital city.

The authorities put together a taskforce dedicated to solving the murders and capturing the killer--whom they dubbed 'The Sadist El Charquito.' However, the bodies stopped turning up. It seemed the killer had ceased his sadistic spree. Although Camargo never openly admitted to these murders, the victimology and methodology both indicate that he was likely responsible. Further strengthening that theory, the killings stopped just when Camargo left Bogotá for Brazil,.

Phase Two

Authorities believe that Daniel Camargo fled Bogotá once he got wind of the special police taskforce. He entered Brazil then travelled along the Amazon River to Manaus, where he attempted to integrate himself by learning to read and speak Portuguese. He used his experience as a door-to-door salesman to go to work selling trinkets on his way to the major cities of Sao Paulo and Rio de Janeiro.

Camargo has not admitted to any murders in Brazil, and there is no solid evidence to tie him to any such acts. His diary entries, however, describe the 'docile' nature of Brazilian women in comparison to the Colombian women he'd victimized, casting suspicion that he may have raped and murdered at least one Brazilian woman in order to draw such a comparison.

In 1973, a Brazilian woman lodged a complaint of fraud against Camargo. While there are no other details available, it is known that the Brazilian authorities immediately captured and deported Camargo to Colombia for his lack of proper documentation. The Brazilian authorities did not wait to receive his Colombian criminal records, releasing him based on his false identity.

Camargo, who was still living under his false identity when he arrived on Colombian soil, decided to move to the Caribbean coast and set himself up in Barranquilla, Colombia. Camargo was forced to live on the streets for the first few months, but he soon found a job as a street vendor selling television monitors. He acquired a black suitcase, which he carried the monitors in, and walked the streets of Sandy hawking his product. Camargo was able to earn a comfortable living and was doing quite well for himself when, one day, he saw a nine-year-old girl while walking past a school. Almost instinctively, Camargo slipped back into his old ways and abducted her. After raping the young girl, Camargo strangled her to death so that she wouldn't be able to 'tattle' to the police as Monica had years before. This murder was Camargo's first confirmed murder. In May of 1974, Camargo was arrested after returning to the scene of a murder where he had accidentally left his suitcase of television screens.

While it is now known that Camargo was responsible for over eighty murders in Colombia, he was convicted for just one -the rape and murder of a nine-year-old. In December 1977, he was interned on the island of Gorgona, Colombia, where he was sentenced to thirty years. The sentence was later reduced to twenty five years—a sentence not consistent with his crimes.

Phase Three

The final phase of Daniel Camargo's evolution encompasses his escape from his island prison and his relentless two-year murder spree in Guayaquil. His escape, the way he manipulated his way back to Ecuador as a free man, is a chilling illustration of how deftly Camargo used his intellectual prowess.

Daniel Camargo's escape from Gorgona is like something out of a film. The heavily guarded prison was located on a remote island, making escape nearly impossible. To this day, the particulars of how Camargo managed to escape are unknown. All that is known for certain is that, in November of 1984, Camargo, after a careful study of the ocean currents surrounding Gorgona, escaped the island on a rickety boat. His escape was considered to be so humiliating that the Colombian authorities initially lied and told the press that Camargo had been eaten alive by sharks.

The rest of the details of Camargo's escape remain a mystery. All that is known for sure is that by the first week of December 1984, Camargo had somehow arrived in Quito, Ecuador, and then travelled on to the densely populated city of Guayaquil by bus, disappearing into its crowded streets. Just weeks later, on 18th December 1984, a nine-year-old girl went missing from the city of Quevedo in Los Rios, Ecuador. Within twenty-four hours of that, a ten-year-old girl was abducted. Was this yet another reign of terror by Daniel Camargo?

The Pursuit of a Psychopath: Chase and Capture

It was 1984. Quito was a bustling city in the heart of Latin America. Ecuador had just begun to heal from the scars that Pedro Alonzo Lopez left on its social landscape. Suddenly, scores of young, attractive women began to go missing in almost all of its major cities. Soon enough, the country was swept up in the same hysteria that it had just put to rest.

For months, the police and the media hunted down every possible lead, and yet nothing made sense. Speculation spread. In hushed whispers, tales of red trucks driven by human-trafficking rings ran rampant. The theory was that these mysterious red trucks were operated by the Ecuadorian Mob, and that the Mob used the trucks to abduct attractive young women and sell them into international prostitution networks. Some claimed the Mob were involved with more than just prostitution; they suspected the abductions to be potentially tied to everything from organ traffickers to sex dungeons, even to satanic cults in which millionaires could purchase the victims as human sacrifices.

It wasn't only vague rumours that were circulating, though. Within weeks, alleged victims began to come forward, and the media broadcasted their statements, in which they claimed to have been abducted by a group of blonde men with heavy Italian accents. These 'victims' went on to claim on public television broadcasts that they had been abducted and taken to ships with foreign flags, where they were then forced to undergo cruel prostitution routines. These statements were so disturbing that they not only incited terror amidst the general public but led to national-level concerns, which led to the government authorising a Navy search and rescue mission along the Pacific coast.

The expedition went on for months, and yet there was no evidence of the 'ghost ship' the victims were describing. The local authorities weren't making much headway with the red truck leads. Desperate, the Civil Defence of the Province of Guayas issued a statement outlining extreme security measures in the face of this yet unidentified threat. The statement required young girls to dress less provocatively, not speak to strangers, and not stay out late at night.

Meanwhile, the people of Ecuador were afraid, and that fear bred animosity. The public began to develop an anti-authoritarian sentiment and take action into their own hands. They decided to search on their own for loved ones, offering rewards within communities, which prompted acts of vigilantism.

Nothing seemed to help. Months passed by, and women kept disappearing.

In 1985, after almost a year without any significant progress, there was a startling development. In the rugged landscape of Guayaquil, piles of female bodies were discovered hidden in a nearly inaccessible section of bush. The bodies were found in groups, stripped naked. There was nothing on them or around them to help identify the victims, but the forensic researchers believed that they had enough evidence to piece together a connection with the missing women of Ecuador.

Within weeks, the forensic team delivered their report. The bodies of all of the women showed signs of asphyxia or strangulation. There were no entry wounds or any other signs of weaponry. There were no bruises other than the strangulation marks inflicted at the time of the murder by the murderer himself. All the bodies indicated that they had been raped at about the same time as they had been murdered.

The forensic team were able to identify the bodies and notify the appropriate family members. During the period of notification, many of the victims' families were reported to have received strange messages and phone calls. Some families even received letters and packages. The person responsible for the murders was taunting them.

In one particular example, a letter was delivered to the family of a young delivery girl, on the Pacific coast, where a group of kidnappers demanded a million sucres ($3,000 USD) in exchange for the young girl. Suspicious, the family demanded proof of life. A few days later, a package arrived for the family. Inside was the underwear of the young delivery girl.

At this point, the family contacted the police, but the messages and phone calls ceased immediately. Even so, the fact that the phone calls had been placed confirmed what the authorities suspected ever since they discovered the bodies hidden in the bushes in Guayaquil.

At this point, the police had already called in renowned Ecuadorian psychiatrist Dr. Oscar Bonilla Leon. Leon reviewed all the available evidence and then used both psychological and sociological profiling to determine that, based on the evidence, it was most likely that the murderer in question would be a man of mature age and average height. Leon went on to dispose of the previous theories of a group or a gang, pointing out that the bodies all showed identical signs of sexual abuse. Strangulation is normally indicative of a single perpetrator. Basic criminology shows that, unlike theft or drug trafficking, sex crimes generally do not involve groups. Given the nature of the crime and the evidence accrued, the most likely scenario was that these disappearances had nothing to do with ghost ships, kidnappings, or human trafficking, but were instead the act of *one* man. Ecuador, once again, had its very own serial killer.

For months, both the Ecuadorian authorities and media used every bit of information they could to keep the people of Ecuador sharp and alert. Finally, this constant vigilance paid off.

One day, a police officer was assisting an old, unfailingly polite man who had fallen down in the middle of the road and, in so doing, dropped a bunch of paperwork. The officer noticed among the paperwork the identity card of a young woman. He didn't think anything of it at the time, but once he was back at the police station, his eyes fell upon the daily newspaper, which published photographs of the most recent victims on its front page. Stunned, the officer felt a chill run down his spine.

This was the same girl whose identification card had fallen out of the old man's documents.

By the time the officer realised that the man was most likely the man they were looking for, it was already nightfall, and he knew there was nothing he could do at that moment. Instead, he waited for daybreak and returned to the sight of the accident. Sure enough, he found the documents that had been scattered across the road the previous day. The evidence was clear. They had found their man.

Based on the documentation collected and a sketch supplied by the Ecuadorian police, a picture of the most wanted man in Ecuador began to circulate. His name was Carlos Solis Bulgarian.

By 1986, there was no police officer in Ecuador who did not know that name. In fact, just weeks later, on February 26th of 1986, two officers patrolling the Avenue of Los Granados de Quito noticed a man limping down the middle of the road, making his way across town with his little black suitcase. The officers later explained that there was something about the way the man's serenity clashed with the bustling little town that prompted them to step forward and ask to check the contents of his suitcase.

Inside the suitcase were a copy of *Crime and Punishment* by Dostoyevsky and the clothes of a young girl. Later, these would be identified as the clothes of eight-year-old Elizabeth Telpes, who had been murdered just two hours before the police came across the limping stranger.

Imprisonment and Death

Dr. Bonilla Leon was the first person to interview the unknown man. After a series of questions, the man claimed to be Carlos Solis Bulgarian, an Ecuadorian who was part of a gang of rapists. Solis went as far as to name his two accomplices, a Jamie Rodriguez and Jorge Chavez. Based on these claims, the suspect was transferred in a police convoy to Guayaquil, where he repeated the same story. The interviewers, however, had already seen the transcripts from the initial interview and noticed that while the suspect stayed true to the theme of his story, there were a number of facts that didn't line up.

For one, the man's accent was not Ecuadorian; it was Colombian. He was constantly mixing up sites and dates. Leon allowed the suspect to weave his way into an immensely tangled web of lies. Once he had, Leon carefully pointed out the discrepancies.

Confronted with such proof of his deceit, the suspect finally showed signs of cracking. The man shifted into the regretful demeanour of a man who had been wronged as much as he had committed wrong, imploring, "Doctor, I just want to know if you would be willing to work with me in the direction of my recovery, to help me return to normal, to return to a useful man."

Well aware of the psychological manipulation that the suspect was attempting to use, Leon agreed and pretended to humour the suspect. It worked. Eventually, the relaxed and admitted, "You're right, I am not Ecuadorian; I am Colombian. And my name is not Carlos Solis Bulgarian. My real name is Daniel Camargo Barbosa."

By the end of the interview, Camargo had admitted to killing and dumping over seventy-one women from Ecuador. He even helped the Ecuadorian authorities find the bodies, and in so doing revealed proof of some of the most sadistic acts of mutilation ever seen on Ecuadorian soil. Camargo's victims had all been girls, but unlike the bodies that had appeared in the bush, these bodies were hacked and crushed. The tortured bodies were barely recognizable. When was asked why he chose young girls, Camargo replied, "Because they cried."

Despite of all the suffering caused by Camargo, he was sentenced to only sixteen years in prison--a sentence that was reduced by two years for 'good behaviour.' Interestingly, one of Camargo's prison mates was Pedro Lopez.

The years rolled by, and the people of Ecuador slowly put behind them horrors of the Charquito. Life as they knew it returned to normal. But this calm was not what it seemed. Back in a corner cell at Quito's Centre for Social Rehabilitation of Men, an inmate, Geovanny Noguera, better known as Luis Masache, was seen to be sharpening his machete. It is said that Masache had come to Guayaquil for the sole purpose of avenging his young niece, who had been one of Camargo's victims. On the 13th November 1994, Masache waited for Camargo to emerge from his cell and delivered twenty blows with his machete. Camargo was left for dead in a pool of his own blood.

Conclusion

A near-continuous campaign of abduction, rape, and murder like the three covered in this book does not happen without massive exploitable gaps and blind spots in important government systems and people's reasoning. In a way, these mass killing sprees may bring about some positive outcomes for the people from the countries they plagued. Communities have become more vigilant, the authorities have greater experience in dealing with such heinous crimes, and the government have had to question how they sentence such crimes. There's a strong argument to suggest that the biggest influence resides with parents. This book exposes the catastrophic effect of a child's neglected and abusive upbringing can have. These 'monsters' are products of the society and culture we have created. The role society plays in each of their lives is critical in moulding who they eventually became.

One wonders: What is more terrifying, the notion that serial killers and child molesters exist and run rampant, that authorities are ill-equipped to deal with such events and deliver just sentences, or that the killers are produced by the failings of society?

About the Author

Ryan Green is an author and freelance writer in his late thirties. He lives in Herefordshire, England with his wife, three children and two dogs. Outside of writing and spending time with his family, Ryan enjoys walking, reading and wind surfing.

Ryan is fascinated with History, Psychology, True Crime, Serial Killers and Organised Crime. In 2015, he finally started researching and writing his own work and at the end of the year he released his first book on Britain's most notorious serial killer - Harold Shipman.

His books are packed with facts, alternative considerations, and open mindedness. Ryan puts the reader in the perspective of those who lived and worked in proximity of his subjects.

Another Title by Ryan Green

Harold Shipman: The True Story of Britain's Most Notorious Serial Killer

Harold Shipman abused his trust as a doctor and used his position to kill – no less than **218 of his patients** found their end at his hand, making him the United Kingdom's most prolific serial killer by a long shot.

This book tells Shipman's story, from his childhood under a domineering mother to his pathetic death in a prison cell.

We make a study of the man's possible motives and close with a look at the systemic failures that allowed him to kill and steps taken to make sure nothing like his murderous spree ever happens again.

Made in the
USA
Middletown, DE